To

Hope you will enjoy this
book on New Zealand-
that there is more than
just Auckland City

Thank you very much
for a thoroughly
stimulating course that
has helped to expand
our horizons.

Hope to see you
return to NZ one
day.

Best Wishes

Helen Krippner

NEW ZEALAND

A O T E A R O A

NEW ZEALAND
A O T E A R O A

PHOTOGRAPHS BY WARREN JACOBS
TEXT BY PETER HOOPER

KOWHAI
PUBLISHING LTD

WATCHER ON THE SHORE

Change comes always from the north,
usually a matter for suspicion,
the first footprint
never returns to the sea.

What gifts do you bring, stranger,
to Tiritiri o te Moana, this land
itself a Gift of the Sea ?
When the first poet saw pohutukawa
he tossed his crimson head-dress
to the wave.

Walking backwards into the future
the tangata whenua see their past
more clearly than those who followed
in the wake of Cook's converted collier
could be sure of their future.

Those first British brought their hopes
and courage but were long
uncertain how to behave in Eden
and darkly they inhabited the land.

We who came by sea
from Hawaiki or Southampton
have now a clearer reckoning
of where we stand
and while nothing is ever dead easy
we could learn to share pride in our land.

To my wife Sally
and my children Grant, Helen and Blair
who continue to give me
encouragement in my vocation

W.J.

Published by Kowhai Publishing Ltd.
299 Moorhouse Ave, Christchurch
10 Peacock Street, Auckland
First published in 1991

Design and finished artwork by
John Burt Graphics, Christchurch

Film positives made in Hong Kong
Printed and bound in Hong Kong

*I gratefully acknowledge the valuable
assistance given by the Department of
Conservation and officers from Te Anau.*

W.J.

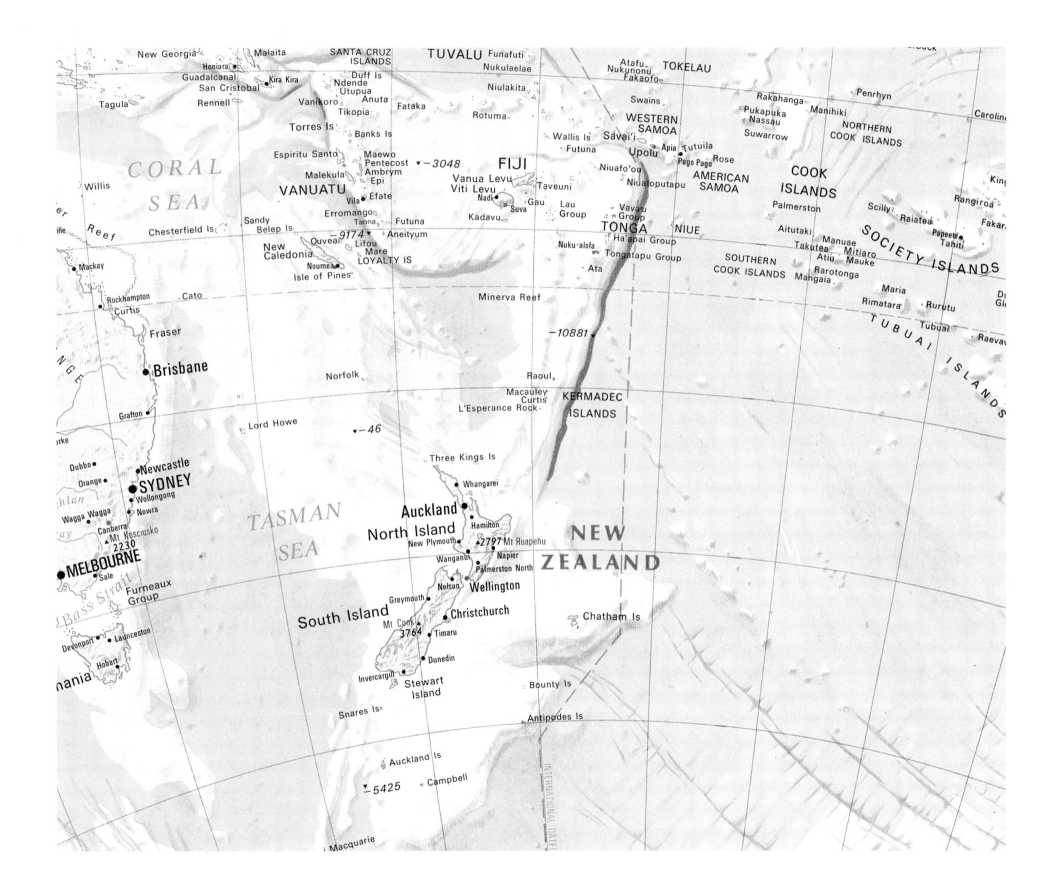

FORESTS

It is summer, the year at its zenith, when clock-driven multitudes surrender to the languors of ocean beach or forest stream. Beyond the conscious escape from urban exhaustion is an unconscious belief in the regenerative powers of non-human energies.

We choose to live apart from nature but are still dimly aware of that larger context of being we forsook long ago, when we chose the apparent certainties of agriculture and social togetherness in place of the physical hazards and hunger of nomadism.

The young, and sometimes even staid adults, respond to the lure of far horizons. We seek a path back down the years to childhood and an imagined time when

> ' each thing was precious for its separateness
> its own ecstactic being'

and when we could

> ' taste again
> the rind-sharp edge of morning.'

Nor the Years Draw Nigh, P. Hooper, Selected Poems

The mathematical imperatives of our urban lives demand precise, logical and rational responses that stifle intuition. Summer may be the only time in the year when energy, will, money and 'just-for-the-kids' sees us drive down the street and steer for the hills. For a while we choose to experience that increasingly rare quality of natural silence that falls like a balm upon bruised and cramped spirits.

We go to the forest to be absorbed, to be enfolded by natural sights and sounds and odours, harmonies of colours and textures in bark and leaf-light and shadow. Ears and eyes begin to focus again upon detail, touch asserts itself as a forgotten pleasure. After a day or two we become again a channel for subtle energies. Serenity becomes possible; we say, 'How peaceful it is.' We have found what we sought, an image of that first garden from which our legendary ancestors were driven.

When Tane Mahuta, in the grief of separating his parents, earth and sky, saw the shivering nakedness of Papa, he mantled her with forest watered by the tears of Rangi, the Sky Father.

Most Kiwis have still to find a nature philosophy that can include the ancient Maori concept of 'mauri', the sacred life force, as well as the teachings of Christianity, but the Green Revolution is already making that amalgam possible. The idea of a living planet, of a life-force throughout nature is accepted not only by many in a spiritual sense but also more and more by scientifically trained minds.

The extraordinary discoveries of modern physics postulate a universe of living energies very much like the intuitive holistic beliefs and practices of the ancient Maori and other cultures of the past. As always, artists and poets foresaw that scientific truth and the essence of beauty would one day be seen as complementary revelations:

> *'Beauty is truth, truth beauty;' - that is all*
> *ye know on earth, and all ye need to know.'*
>
> Ode on a Grecian Urn, John Keats

But -

> *'There is a very unfortunate tendency in our*
> *era to imagine that nature is reverie, laziness*
> *and languor.'*
>
> Michelet, The Mountain.

Serious artists have never made the mistake - the canvases of Toss Woollaston constantly emphasize the energies of nature in mountain and water forces; "The Bone People" is a rugged boulder of only partly disciplined power; the pots of Yvonne Rust match the challenging energies of the potter herself.

Thus the two main islands of New Zealand exhibit different kinds of energies. In the North Island human settlement hovers always on the brink of threats of volcanic disruption - is it fanciful to see its people as more volatile and mercurial than those of the South, where society is founded upon a more stable and geologically ancient land?

Be that valid or not, it is true that the whole country is a matrix of vast energies, chthonic and climatic, which have their counterparts in human energies; we are much given to the tussles of confrontation; certainly physical - is there a rising creative mental component in our culture? I'd like to think so.

Have you ever sat listening to music while watching a strong wind plunging through a forest? Inrushing floods of air set the whole forest into wild rhythms that parallel symphonic music.

Recently while listening to Sibelius, (the symphonic poem Tapiola), I sat watching a tide of nor'west wind flowing over rainforest. Tapio is the Forest God of Finnish mythology, and while his mysterious dusky realms are not our colourful bushland, under the spell of the music, I was caught up in the magic of that universal dance where art becomes, not a mimicry of nature, but a natural energy in its own right.

Knowing a forest is much more than merely looking at it or stepping into its shade; it means becoming possessed by its spirit, to be rocked on the winds of Pentecost. And it requires a most delicate balance between the knowledge of science and humility between the magical symbiosi which is the natural world's expression of love. Kneel, and marvel at the fragile beauty of cordyline pumilio, the pigmy cabbage tree, and look upwards to be drenched by the heady perfumes of spring blossom in the great cordyline australis.

If you would plant grace in your spring garden, delight it by growing drifts of rengarenga, the rock lily; if you would ennoble farm or park, establish a kauri tree.

In the Waipoua Forest the kauri, Tane Mahuta, was a sapling when Christ was born and New Zealand was a forest of arboreal temples ringing with bird song.

Kauris older and larger than Tane Mahuta have been recorded, their stumps six metres or more across. Today, to walk a forest track in Northland one can still reach a mosaic of grey-brown scales and be amazed and humbled to find a wall of wood towering over the centuries. Throughout the country the most splendid trees of our remaining forest are the great podocarps - kauri, totara, rimu, matai, kahikatea.

At 50 metres or more, the latter is our tallest native tree, now found in significant stands only in South Westland.

Their height is best appreciated seen along river flats lifting above a canopy of smaller growth. As single specimens in an open space they may acquire a denser branching habit than when competing with others of the species in close-set stands.

It is the smaller shrubs, saplings, climbers and trees which give most immediate visual pleasure to the visitor, especially in spring and summer. Throughout the spring countryside dark stands of forest may be graced by shawls of star-fallen clematis individsa. Our national flower, the kowhai, is most attractive on a stream bank or edging a lake.

A lowland or hillside kamahi forest in spring and summer will be a flourish of creamy-pink candle-blooms, the later dried seed-stalks a pleasing rusty tinge.

Succeeding the kamahi will come the lily-of-the-valley-scented flowers of the hinau, common in regenerating forest.

Too often unregarded, heathlands ghost-grey with manuka repay a close examination of the five-petalled, free-flowering shrub throughout most of the summer. And what a pleasure it is to find at the forest edge of a campsite a grove of slender ribbonwood or lacebark, their creamy-white blossoms cooling a summer day. Or to find October's sweet-scented kaikomako ripening its purple berries in May.

Creeper or bushy shrub, the white flowering rata can persist through December into February, the liane very pretty when it clusters about the stump of a naked ponga.

Of all the country's flowering native trees, mature pohutukawa and related northern rata, are the most spectacular. Along the western slopes of the Alps, the southern rata once smouldered summer through, but has now been devastated by opposums, high ridges of rata now stark with dead trees. I shall never again see those forests as once I saw them on a long summer drive through the ruby heartland of the great island.

Young children may reap their best rewards from the floor of the forests, and are more likely than adults to exclaim in delight at tiny white-winged panakenake - and get their shoes damp as they crouch to examine the treasure.

It was Housman who lamented that
' to look at things in bloom
Fifty springs are little room.'

Do Kiwis need to be reminded that in rainforest or the darker austere beauty of beech woods, there is always the magic of seasonal change to alert attention? Every day forests reveal new aspects of their beauty.

Stars slowly lifting into a night sky over a forested ridge are a measure of time as miraculous as centuries of epiphitic growth hosted by the most venerable rimu that overlooks valleys and hills of the seasoned world.

plates: 1 - 21

All action taken to protect our forest is self-fulfillment in our own time and an earnest of gratitude from posterity.

MOUNTAINS RIVERS AND LAKES

In 1987, for various complex reasons, the Tuwharetoa people gifted the peaks of Ruapehu, Ngauruhoe and Tongariro to the Crown as our first National Park. Its features exemplify the complex forces of nature which create volcanic landscapes. In Tongariro for example the powers of ice and fire are in perpetual conflict, forming and destroying shapes of terror and beauty.

Yet even there at the throne of the winds, the lesson is constantly hammered home that life will not be denied - algae and lichen soon begin to colonise cooled lava flows.

Only the most intrepid of spirit and stubborn of physical strength should venture into these regions. There is a spiritual dimension in the ascent of a mountain, but to stand on the lip of a smouldering crater involves awe and a stirring of primitive fear. Burning mountains confront us with terrestrial powers prior to the origins of life, yet people have cultivated the lower slopes of many active volcanoes for thousands of years.

Religion and science look behind and beyond, yet our brief individual lives hope and long for immortality. A mountain provides us with an image of the eternal. Within the ambit of mountain images our human frailties are both humbled and assured of strength.

Many of us have our own familiar mountain within easy access from home. Years of familiarity endear its character to us and we fiercely resent any unwarranted intrusion into its sacred solitudes. It need not be one of the land's grandest peaks, but a level to which we can ascend when our souls are in need of affirmation and refreshment.

For me, it has always been Mount Davy, barely 1200 metres high at the southern end of the Paparoa Range along 100 kilometres of dramatic marine highway between Greymouth and Westport. As a boy growing up on a farm at the foot of the mountain I was conscious always of a mysterious fastness beyond familiar paddocks. In winter the plateau peak was briefly blanketed in snow, summer sunsets flushed their last colours upon its breadth.

Coal mines bored into the lower slopes, sawmills had eaten into beech forest. Only further north along the coastal highway began the rainforest which today draw tourists to the richly diverse attractions of the Paparoa National Park.

In the 'thirties' I used to stand on the pedals of a push-bike for five kilometres along the railway line up to Rewanui, before climbing a steep face to a ridge until the bush opened out to dwarf shapes and the tussock plateau. North along the ridge, Croesus Track twisted another twenty kilometres to Barrytown, eastwards stretched the Grey Valley and far to the south the Alps curved beyond Cook and Tasman over the horizon.

I peopled the summit of Mount Davy with the Greek heroes of Charles Kingsley's imagination, of Perseus and Andromeda, who at death were translated into star patterns of the night sky:

"All night long they shine for a beacon to wandering sailors; but all day they feast with the gods on the still blue peaks of Olympus."

Why do we climb mountains if not to attain those lyrical heights of the self we rarely attain in the denser atmospheres of every day?

The green countrysides of Taranaki and Westland, lush in grass and forests, their mountains athwart the Tasman's westerlies, are always copiously watered. Configurations of road and rail are determined by the short swift rivers, so unlike the wide shallow river valleys of Canterbury that have formed the country's most extensive plains.

Centuries of myth and legend make the beautiful Wanganui River sacred to the Maori. In spite of its waters being drained by massive hydro projects, only in recent years has legislation begun to protect some of our wild and scenic rivers.

Water is life. Until recently we could truthfully tell visitors that our river waters were all safe to drink; sadly, discoveries of the virus giardia mean this may no longer be true. Even these sweet waters at the end of the world are being polluted.

Yet for climber and deer stalker, artist and camping Kiwi, the mountain streams will continue to make a liquid music through dappled shade. No other aspect of nature is more beautiful, more serenely satisfying, more spiritually uplifting, than a blend of dancing light and shade over rippling water. Given the chance, who would not choose to establish a home beside a forest stream? Such influences can parallel the course of a stream with the course of a human life.

"A River Rules My Life" by Mona Anderson, first published in 1963, is the classic study of how the Rakaia River determines life on the back country sheep station of Mount Algidus in Canterbury. Erosion and aggradation are clearly still carving the surface of the land, but human ingenuity taps their waters for hydro-electric power and tames them into irrigation channels for the crops of dry farmlands.

However, our country remains blessed by thousands of streams trickling from cold mountain summits, leaping giddily from precipitous bluffs or winding at leisure down valleys and across plains to mingle sweet waters with salt, at the shore of Tasman or Pacific.

Equally enchanting in mountainous landscapes are the country's numerous lakes - from far-famed Taupo in the north to the deep narrow lakes of Fiordland.

They are usually far from industrial activity, very often in settings of great natural beauty. Lakes always take the traveller by the heart - "Oh, look! There's the lake." At once we are in a different relationship with the world.

The solid surface of the earth may wear a forbidding aspect, a lake, almost never. There, in shining abundance, is the ultimate need of all life, water, the symbol of salvation, the restorer of peace to the weary heart, play and laughter and delight for the innocent.

The mood of a lake may change from hour to hour. From the mists of early day the slow wing-beat of a heron pulses with the essence of serenity, miniscule ripples on a pebbly shore are the thought of a thousand poets. The fringing trees of a lake shore acquire mystery from reflection in clear water; an indented shoreline is a lure to the faraway of all journeys.

plates: 22 - 61

And no lake water has more depth of power in it than a mountain tarn. Encrusted rocks at the edge of the water are the physical reality of reflected peaks. In the depths of a tarn three eternities meet, rocks and water and sky. In the presence of that infinite loneliness we can offer only silence.

fourteen

FARMLANDS

We live now in a period of rapid change in farming methods forced upon us by diminishing returns from former markets. The appearance of the countryside is changing as remnants of native forests are protected in farmland, trees are planted for shelter and beauty, dark pine forest mantle the hills, new crops and market gardens specialize in exotic species and hundreds of small organic farms rely upon natural instead of chemical fertilisers.

Textures, colours and patterns of land use vary from the brick-coloured volcanic soils of Pukekohe market gardens, through 1500 kilometres of latitude to the rolling green downlands of Southland. It takes a month or six weeks for the tides of spring to flow down the country from the 'winterless' north to the Alexandra Blossom Festival in October.

Substantial homes of Waikato dairy farmers usually set amidst pleasant gardens reflect the wealth of their deep green pastures. The cultivation of lower hill slopes often leaves remnant forests clothing the summits, appropriate to the English term 'hanging woods'.

Most people would admit to enjoying the sight of prosperous farmland whether in crops or pasture. The satisfaction of seeing land well cared for goes very deep a long way back to the beginnings of civilisation. To belong to the land, in its bone and spirit, is to belong to the cycle of seasons, to be a necessary part of life itself. Wanderers though we are, for most of us some part of this varied country is called home.

Variety is very much part of the cultivated beauty of the Nelson province where intensive cropping and market gardening give a range of textures to a well-watered landscape. Well-preserved Victorian farmhouses in remoter districts challenge the artist's eye to catch the echo of history, both in house and Lombardy poplar introduced by early settlers.

Farm gates can linger long in the memory and give specific local character to a region. Last century a few country mansions of the squirarchy featured massive stone pillars with wrought iron gates, but no longer appropriate to a diminished kingdom.

Venerable wooden gates are especially attractive, their lichened timbers and rasping hinges still telling of laden hay wagons and the lingering farewells of country lovers. A whole book could be given to country gates and the memories they invoke.

Or, less seriously, a rustic tale centred upon the hilarities of Dad and Dave urging a refractory bull through a Taranaki gate - are there today urban youngsters who don't know what a Taranaki gate is?

To fly over the Canterbury Plains is to realise how precisely the demands of commerce can regulate landscape. From the air the prospect is one of undeviating mathmatical precision, until the eye rests gladly upon one of the region's four great rivers.

plates: 62 - 96

Always in the background are the Alps, under sunset cloud or a cover of snow. And somewhere, inevitably, thousands of Canterbury lambs.

Few travellers penetrate as far inland as the vast sheep stations of the interior. These regions stand apart, physically isolated by rivers and lonely in the greater loneliness of the mountains. The lean and casual musterer, laconic of word and sparing of his strength on the tops, lives out his work in a landscape of heroic proportions. Few men and women choose to live in the high country, but those who leave it will be forever haunted by its harsh beauties.

Between ocean and land there is eternal give-an-take as a stretch of sandy coast is eaten into, shallow estuaries become silted. Those who live near the sea share in both elements. Much inhuman life is imposed upon us, we constantly adjust to influences we did not choose. Our lives, as Thoreau points out, "are frittered away by detail" but whatever influences the sea might bring us - powerful, grand, sublime, tragic, they are never trivial. Along seashores we relate to the deeper levels of our natures.

On a long empty shingle beach I wonder at the whys and wherefores of life:

" The Sea of Faith
Was once, too, at the full...
But now I only hear
Its melancholy, long, withdrawing roar...
... down the vast edges drear
and naked shingles of the world."

Dover Beach, Mathew Arnold.

Most New Zealander's live near the sea in a land which is nowhere more than 120 kilometres from a beach. Nearly all our main towns and cities are near the sea. Auckland's magnificent Waitemata harbour could hold all the navies of the world - a City of Sails in very truth, its Anniversary Days celebrated by regattas of a thousand yachts.

Every kind of seaside recreation is available to most Kiwis, from lazing in summer sunshine on hot sands, swimming, surfing, yachting - is it any wonder that we excel at the latter? From cleaving the waters of the world's vast oceans to "simply" messing about in boats, the health-giving beaches of our indented coastlines have entered deeply into our national consciousness.

As the Green Revolution alerts us ever more sharply to the values, physical and spiritual, of these beautiful islands, we are treating with more respect beaches, river-mouths, parks and reserves along our coasts. Pollution of coastal waters, especially near large centres of population will continue to face communities and governments with major challenges.

Northward from Auckland, bay, headland and estuary are only lightly sprinkled with settlement - if one excepts Whangarei. There is a splendid loneliness about the Ninety Mile Beach over the sandhills of Te Paki to the glittering silica sand of Spirits Bay, but vast solitudes of seacoast are more common to the South Island.

The drowned valleys of the Marlborough Sounds possess a serenity which can accept human settlement but one hopes that their shores will never be substantially "developed."

Very different are the tall solitudes of Fiordland, where only the gods of mountains, forests and storms naturally reign. Mountains that plunge vertically into the sea tolerate only the merest nicks and scratches of human ways, but no one who visits Fiordland can fail to be awed by their majesty. Recent World Heritage status for the whole of south-western New Zealand is a recognition of its unique natural qualities.

One man alone has seen all the coasts of New Zealand by deliberate choice from a frail canoe a few kilometres off-shore, during remarkable voyages around the country's three main islands. He is Paul Caffyn, West Coast geologist, mountaineer and canoeist, his unparalleled feats deserving of much wider recognition than provided by his own modest, though lively, accounts.

Over a decade beginning in the late seventies, Paul not only paddled thousands of kilometres along all New Zealand's shores, but did the same for Britain, Australia, Japan and along Alaskan coasts.

A Magic Kiwi like no other.

PETER HOOPER

plates: 97 - 126

COLOUR PLATES

FORESTS

I should not have thought
so many greens harmonious
though the poet Marvell wrote
' a green thought in a green shade'
and he was right:
frond greens of fern, leaf showers
of kiekie, the wristy twist
of flaxes under wind.
                              Pillars
of branching trunks grey-greened
by drooping epiphytes.
Green moving canopies
high over glooms and glades
of emerald translucency,
green ... green harmonies all
in a music of green lives.

1 Matai tree, South Westland

2 Rimu bark, Brod Bay, Fiordland National park

3 Kauri bark, Trounson Kauri Park

4 Tree ferns, Rotorua

5 Morning mist, Lake Mapourika

6 Moss, Westland rain forest

7 Trout stream, Rotorua

8 Stream near Kumara, Westland

Blue pools, Aspiring National Park

10 Limestone, Paparoa National Park

11   Fox River cave, Paparoa National Park

12　Icicles, Arthurs Pass

13   Purakanui Falls, Southland

14   Beech forest, Lake Mavora

15   Kauri forest, Trounson Kauri Park

16   Rainbow, Fox Glacier   17   The Chasm, Cleddau Valley, Fiordland National Park

18   Marble outcrops, Takaka hill

19 Caples Valley, Fiordland

20 Sub-alpine beech forest, Key Summit, Fiordland

21 Moss and ferns in beech forest

MOUNTAINS RIVERS AND LAKES

Far other Presences than ours
delight in thrones and powers
of these high places,
granite tombs make time itself
lichened past all change -
         but, no,
amongst the windy tussock
mosses and herbs suck fragile
beauty from the wraiths of cloud
traversing Buckland Peaks,
and waters from sweet tarns
ooze, trickle, gather, leap
to urge green valleys broader,
gouge them deep.
         Waters and rocks:
ages and seasons cradle earth
to flower in silences - oh, look!
among these twisted roots
an alpine gentian!

22   Routeburn Valley, Fiordland National Park

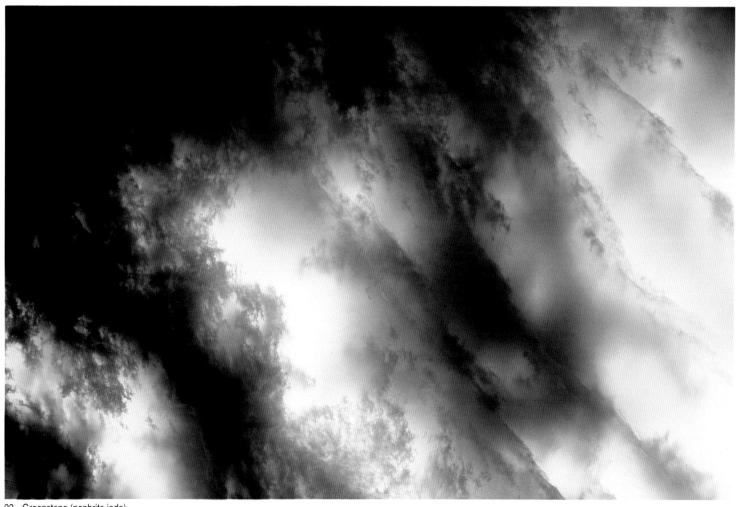

23 Greenstone (nephrite jade)

24 Moturau Bay, Manapouri

25   Mackenzie Country winter

26 Lake Rotorua sunrise

27 Mitre Peak, Milford   28 Mt. Cook Lily

29 Lake Tekapo in winter

30 North-west wind shaped clouds, Fairlie

31 Westland valley and Tasman Sea

32 Lindis Pass hill patterns

33   Fox Glacier & Fritz Range, Westland National Park

34 Kaikoura Ranges

35   Red Stag roar, Lilybank Station

36   Richmond Range, Tekapo

37   Waimakariri River & Canterbury Plains

38   Winter, Canterbury High Country

39   Sulphur Point, Lake Rotorua

40   Lake Tekapo

41   Lake Alexandrina   42   Lake Matheson dawn

43 Lindis Pass

44   Lake Tekapo

45 Glendhu Bay,   46 White Heron (Kotuku)

47 Mackenzie Country winter

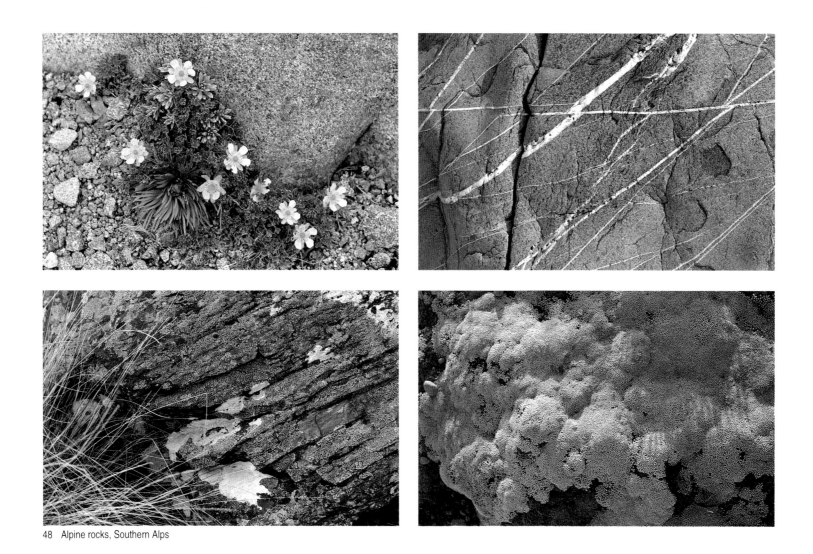

48 Alpine rocks, Southern Alps

49 Richmond Station and Range

50 Lake Taupo & Motutaiko Is

51 Aorero River, West Nelson

52   Wairere Stream, Waikato

53   Hoar-frost, Lake McGregor

54   Breeze on shore, Lake McGregor

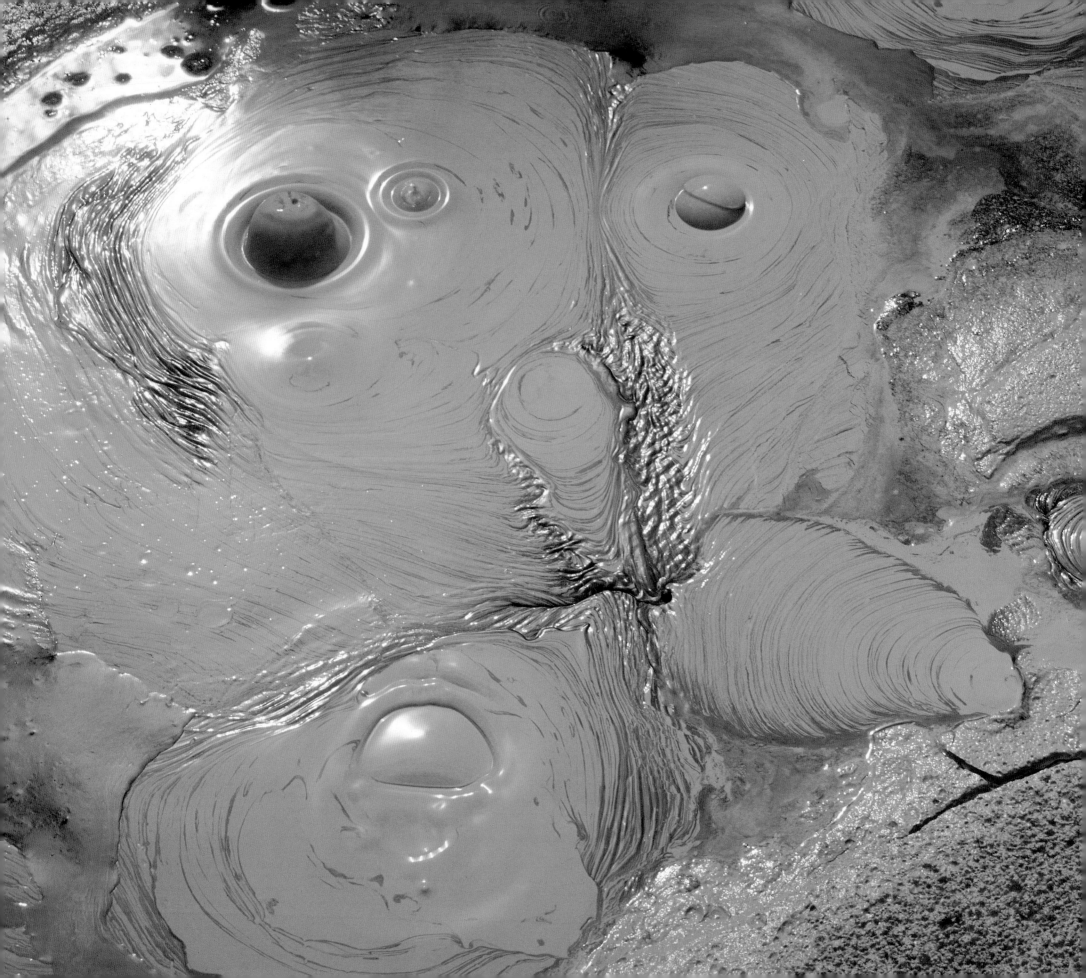

55 Boiling mud, Wairakei Valley   56 Pohutu Geyser, Whakarewarewa

57   58

59   60 Geothermal patterns   61 White Island crater

FARMLANDS

Many of us can look back
to some farmer in the family,
Sargeson's Uncle Oakley or the like
breaking in hill country
near Taumaranui. Only recently
we've scraped the dung off our boots.

It was cold in a rainy sunrise
rounding up a dozen cows
to be milked by hand
for town supply, knocking
bobby calves on the head
that couldn't be given away.

Wet summers when hay rotted
before autumn yellowed the poplars
but also times when the last load
crammed the barn full - 'You kids
keep out, no jumping in it, hear?'
and late after dusk
the separator droned of cream.

Grey loosened weatherboards hide
only the emptiness of has-been,
blackberries choke roses by the creek,
in the orchard leaning apple-trees
and bearded with lichen, tho' spring
still manages nostalgia
to push daffodils through the mud.

62 Farmland Pukeatua, Waikato

63   Tractor working field near Geraldine

64   Tukituki Valley, Hawkes Bay

65   Gwavas landscape, Hawkes Bay

66   Fairlie pastoral

67   Evening light, Burkes Pass

68   Sun's rays, Stoke Valley

69 After the rain, Taupo   70 Choumoullier crop, Clydevale, Southland

71 Lindis Valley, North Otago

72   Arrow Basin in winter

73   French Pass road, Marlborough

74   Evening Manuherikia Valley, Otago

75 Lucerne crop, Lake Hayes

76   Broadlands, Waikato

77   South of Te Kuiti

78 Clouds, Takaka Valley

79   Lake Wakatipu pastoral

80   Farm shed, Wakefield

81   South Canterbury hill pattern

82   Te Waewae Bay, Southland

83   Waitaki Valley

84 Kaitorete Spit from Banks Peninsula

85   Hikurangi from Hiruharama, East Coast

86   Morven Hills historic woolshed (above)

87   Morning dew on grass

88   Plane trees, Lake Victoria, Christchurch

89 Waipukurau farmscape

91 Morning fog, Moeraki

92   Haymaking, Arrow Basin

93   Geraldine hills

94   Rape crop, Canterbury Plains

95   Lockett Range, West Nelson

96   Hanmer Forest

COASTS

Always the long sea murmurs
under our sleep, we are never far
from that other who waits in us
to worship the sun, lift with the
racing wave and be spent on the shore.

A beach unmasks the week of all pretence
releases workers to their bodies' ease
at Piha, Oriental Bay or Kerikeri,
or to coasts' surprises further south
exploding seas upon the Pancake Rocks,
Moeraki Boulders - boy! some turtle eggs!

Humanity is here: labourer from
the steelworks, apprentice market gardener,
the girl from the boutique, mum
and the kids, students taking the sun,
Old Pop and little Emma scuffing sand.

Consciously or not all must accept
the absolution of the moving tides.

97 Tahunanui shore, Nelson

98   Bay of Islands from Rawhiti

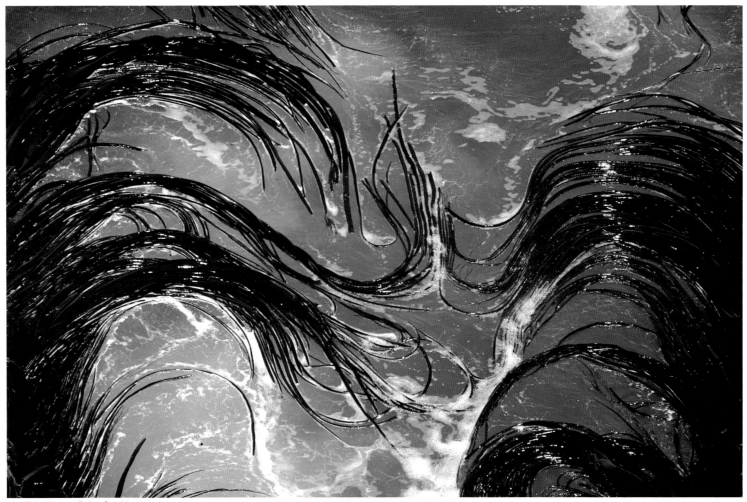

99   Kelp, Nugget Point, Southland

100 Taylors Bay, Mahia   101 Nikau Palm frond, Karamea

102 Opoutama Beach, Hawke Bay

103 Cabbage trees, Pelorous Sound

104 Spirits Bay, Northland

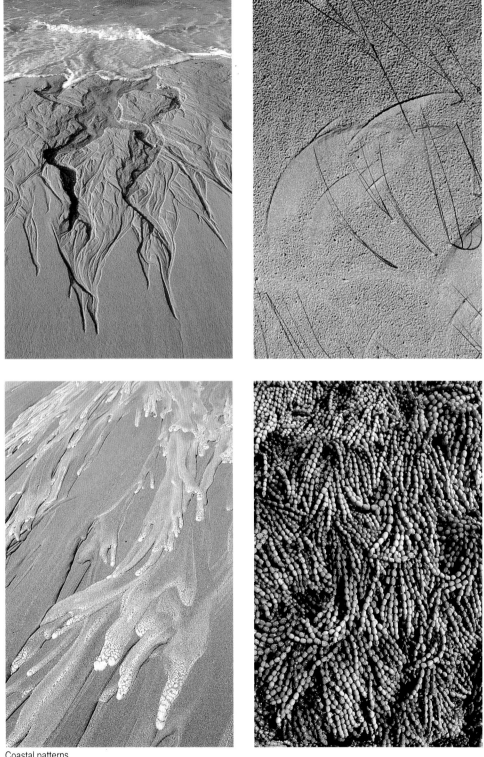

105 106

107 108
Coastal patterns

109 Te Waewae Bay at Orepuki

110   Arnott Point and Tasman Sea, South Westland

111 Dusky Sound from Indian Island

112 Riverton fishing boats

113   Wharariki Beach, Nelson west coast

114   Iron sands, Tongaporutu, Taranaki

115   Port Pegasus, Stewart Island

116   Patterson Inlet, Stewart Island

117 Shag Rock, Sumner, Christchurch

118   Terns, Rakaia River mouth

119 Morning mist, Warrington Coast, Otago

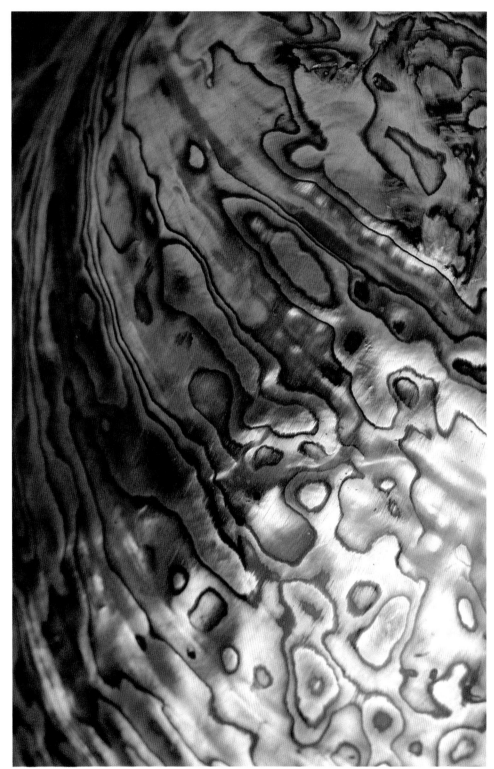

120   Paua shell detail

121 Blacks Beach, Hawke Bay

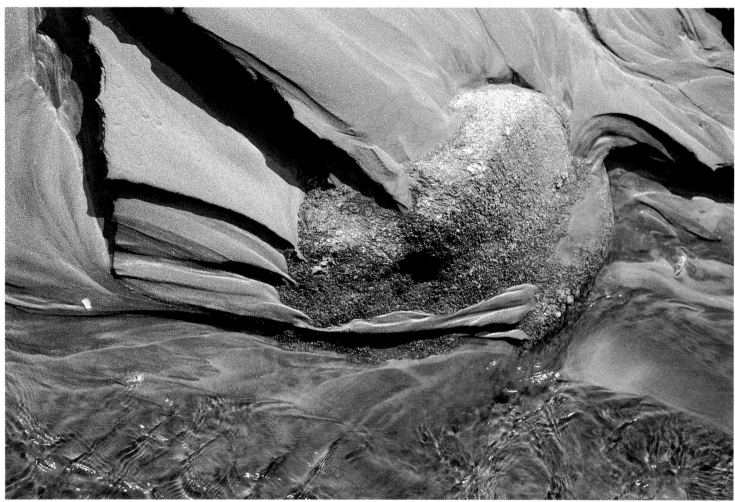

122   Charleston Beach, Westland

123 Punakaiki Coast

124   Rock pool, Waipapa Point, Southland

125   Tidal mud flats, Catlins Lake

126   Dusky Sound, Fiordland National Park